I SPY
TRUCKS
with my little eye

Ages 2-5

Little Cat Press

Welcome to Little Cat Press, where learning and playing come together in the most delightful way!

From coloring books to activity books, our high-quality books engage young readers in fun and educational activities. They encourage creativity and thinking skills while helping children identify with the world around them. Little Cat Press is dedicated to providing hours of entertainment and learning for kids of all ages.

Embark on a journey of discovery and adventure through our wonderful world of books, and help your child unlock the joy of reading and learning with Little Cat Press!

LITTLE
CAT
PRESS

LITTLE
CAT
PRESS

This book belongs to

_____

_____

_____

I spy with my little eye some red trucks. Can you spot them all?

There are four red trucks in total.

I spy with my little eye a truck starting with the letter

B

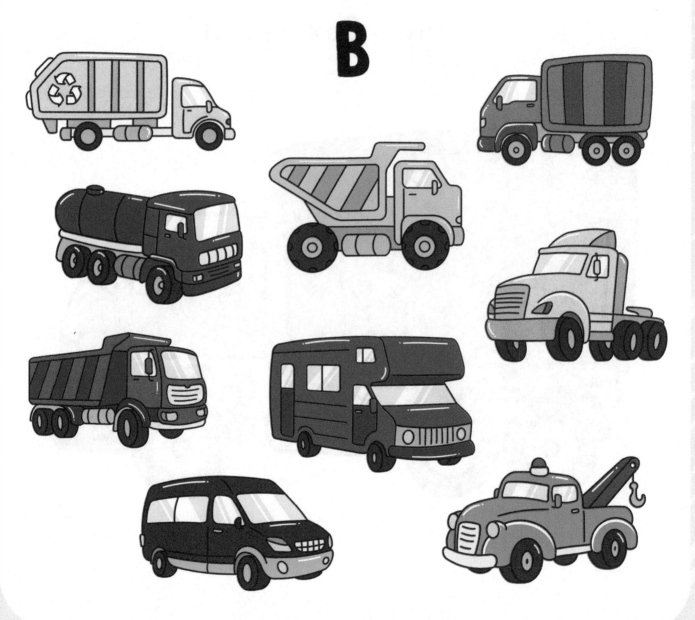

I spy a Box Truck!

Are there more  or  ?

There are more green concrete mixer trucks than orange vans.

4

3

I spy with my little eye a truck starting with the letter

D

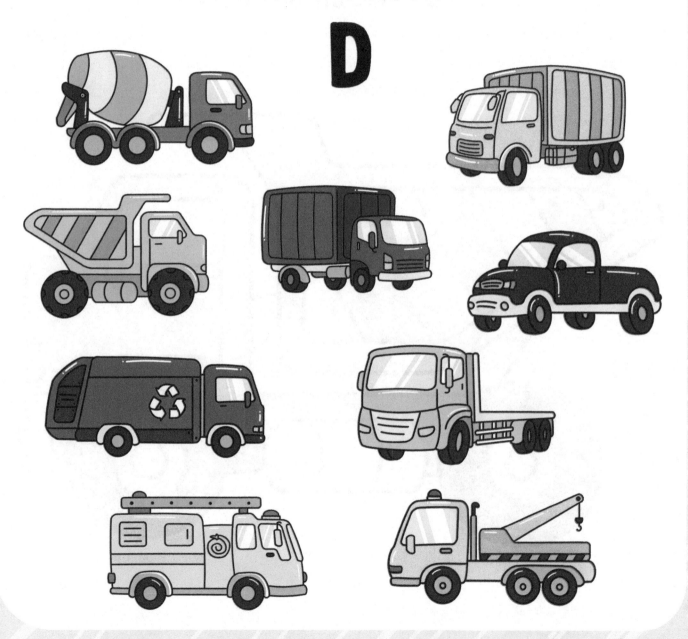

I spy a Dump Truck!

Find and count all the trucks that look like this one.

There are three dump trucks that look like this one!

I spy with my little eye a truck starting with the letter

F

I spied a Flatbed Truck!

I spy with my little eye two pink trucks.
Can you spot them all?

Here they are, the pink van and the pink recreational vehicle!

I spy with my little eye some trucks that look like this one. Can you spot them all?

There are four monster trucks that look like this one!

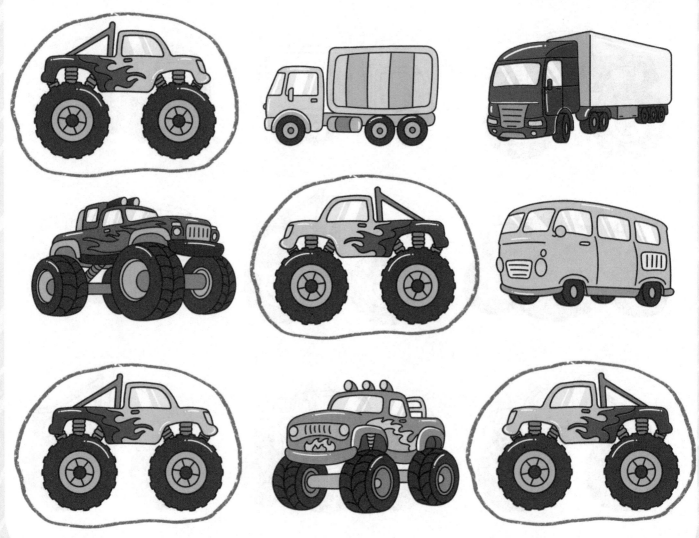

I spy with my little eye a truck starting with the letter

T

I spied a Tanker Truck!

I spy with my little eye some brown trucks. Can you spot them all?

There are five brown trucks in total.

I spy a truck with a color that begins with the letter

G

Here it is, the grey concrete mixer truck!

Can you find two trucks that look the same?

These two tractor units look alike!

Find and count all the trucks that look like this one.

There are three vans that
look like this one!

I spy a truck with a color that begins with the letter

B

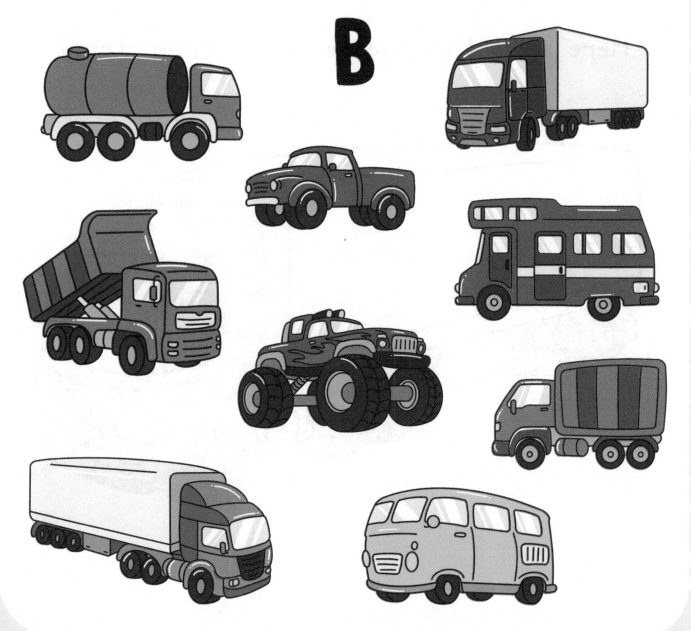

Here it is, the blue semi – trailer truck!

Are there more  or  ?

There are more red dump trucks
than pink vans.

3

2

I spy with my little eye two trucks that look the same. Can you find them?

These two box trucks look alike!

I spy with my little eye a yellow truck. Can you find it?

Here it is, the yellow tanker truck!

I spy with my little eye some fire trucks. Can you spot them all?

There are three fire trucks in total.

I spy with my little eye a truck starting with the letter

P

I spied a Pickup Truck!

Are there more  or  ?

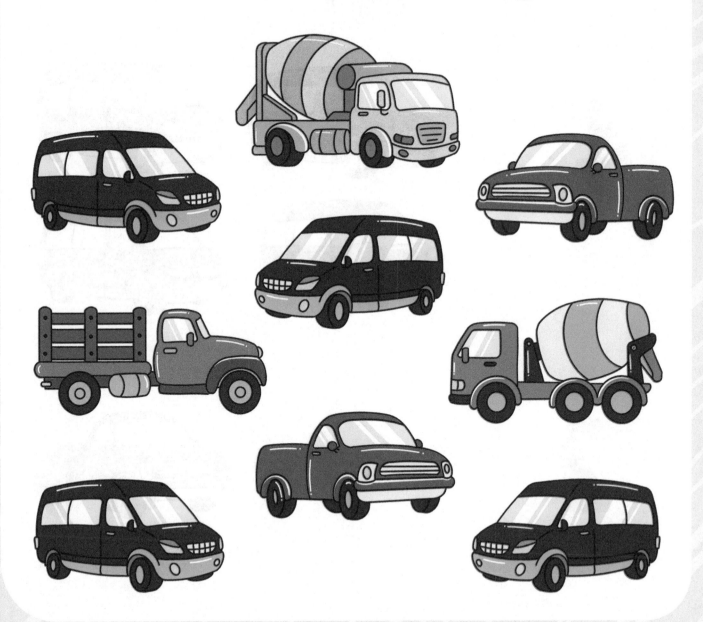

There are more **black vans** than
pink pickup trucks.

4

2

Can you find two trucks that look the same?

These two concrete mixer trucks look alike!

Find and count all the trucks that look like this one.

There are two dump trucks that look like this one!

I spy with my little eye some yellow trucks.
Can you spot them all?

There are five yellow trucks in total.

I spy with my little eye a truck starting with the letter

S

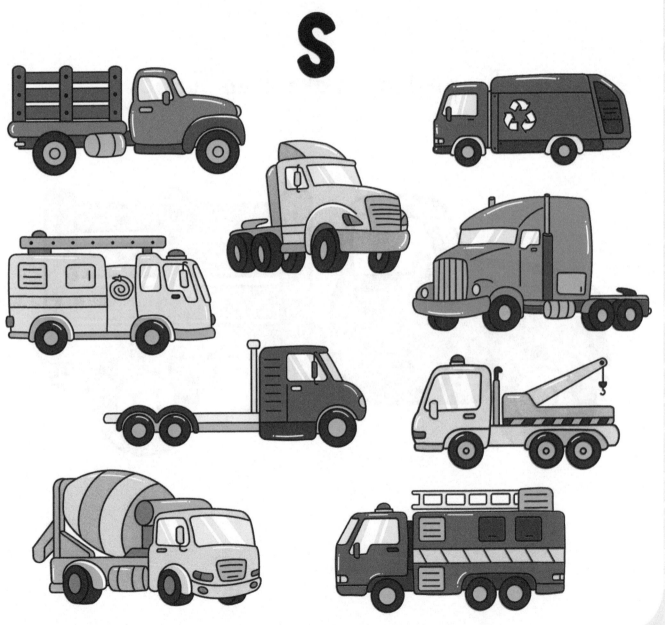

I spied a Stake Bed Truck!

I spy with my little eye some Semi - Trailers. Can you spot them all?

There are three Semi-trailers in total.

Are there more  or  ?

There are more monster trucks than dump trucks.

5

3

I spy with my little eye a truck starting with the letter

T

I spied a Tow Truck!

I spy with my little eye some green trucks.
Can you spot them all?

There are five green trucks in total.

Can you find two trucks that look the same?

These two box trucks look alike!

I spy with my little eye a truck starting with the letter

G

I spied a Garbage Truck!

Find and count all the trucks that look like this one.

There are six yellow tanker trucks that look like this one!

I spy a truck with a color that begins with the letter

P

Here it is, the purple recreational vehicle!

Congratulations! You did it!
You've completed the I Spy Trucks Book!

We hope you had a fantastic time exploring the interactive pages, filled with exciting challenges and surprises. You've done an excellent job of sharpening your observation skills and developing your cognitive abilities. Keep up the good work, and we look forward to seeing you embark on many more thrilling adventures in the future!

Truck Collection

Box Truck

Flatbed Truck

Dump Truck

Semi-Trailer Truck
(Tractor-Trailer)

Pickup Truck

Truck Collection

Garbage Truck

Tanker Truck

Tow Truck

Fire Truck

Concrete Mixer Truck

Truck Collection

Recreational Vehicle

Monster Truck

Stake Bed Truck

Van

Tractor Unit

Made in the USA
Las Vegas, NV
01 March 2024

86557130R00044